Haying the far fields

The Year the Bears Invaded Duluth

THEY MUST HAVE descended from the night sky,
Ursa Major emptied,
whipped in on the winds of space.
Or maybe across the frozen straits
from the Steppes,
lean and hungry,
the winter having been too long.

They swarmed the dumps,
pawing through the fetid leavings,
raided root cellars,
lumbered like scraggly drunks
through all the best neighborhoods.

When I rode with Grandpa to town,
we'd see at least three
bears treed, the crowds below
circling like dogs
ready to close in for the kill,
keeping them there
to wait for the bear truck.

Sometimes four or five would wade
slow, as if grass were water,
into our orchard,
would rear up to take the green apples,

sour juice dripping,
narrow eyes squeezed a little in pleasure.
Oh it was good, you could tell,
and they kept returning
despite Uncle Odd,
who ran like an avenger up the hill,
his rifle firing wildly.

One sleepy morning a bear
walked bold as berries
through the revolving door
of the Hotel Duluth.
Imagine his consternation,
people like a flock of startled birds
except the one man reading the paper
who heard nothing.

By the time a small one wandered
into our blacksmith shop,
I'd gotten used to them.
Uncle Gunnar shut the door
and called the game warden.
I pressed my nose to the window
to see the bear, he pressed his
next to mine – two pointy noses,
four curious eyes.

If angry Uncle hadn't swept me up,
would he have broken that pane,
reached for me?

I never thought so.
He seemed as curious as I,
so out of his element
he thought perhaps he was dreaming
of a ghost girl falling
into the well of his eyes,
or the surprise smell
of iron and rust, old harness,
the acrid bite of coal dust
that puffed like powder
with each shuffling step.

By winter they were gone,
the apples they had left uneaten
were mounded and cidery
in our root cellar.
The bears of the north sky remained
bright and mythic, predictable
as the snow that swept the roofs
of the houses below.

Haying the far fields

POEMS ON A MINNESOTA CHILDHOOD

E L L A   E Y T A N

a grassroots book

N

TRUE NORTH PRESS
SAN ANSELMO, CALIFORNIA

FIRST EDITION

Some of the poems herein previously appeared, in earlier versions,
in the following publications:

Barnabe Mountain Review 4 (1998–99): "Stereopticon"

Grrrrr: A Collection of Poems About Bears (C. B. Follett, ed.;
Arctos Press, 2000): "The Year the Bears Invaded Duluth,"
"Down-Home Cooking"

Loonfeather (Fall–Winter 1994): "The Old Einbu Farm,"
"Blacksmithing"

Marin Poetry Center Anthology 2 (1999): "The Year the Bears
Invaded Duluth"

For information about the Grassroots Series, please write to:
Robin Jacobson, Publisher / True North Press
308 Laurel Avenue, San Anselmo, California 94960-2111
or email: truenorthpress@home.com

ISBN 0-9709705-0-1

Printed & bound in the United States of America

I DEDICATE THIS BOOK TO MY FAMILY

Matt, Elana, and David
for their interest in and support of the project

Wesley, my brother and fellow traveler
through those Minnesota years

and my mother, father, grandparents, aunts, and uncles
who, with their various gifts for living
inspired these poems

Contents

Haying the far fields

Stereopticon

THE IMAGE appears doubled
until I clip it to the pole
and peer through paired lenses.
Suddenly, everything
is dimensional.
Light puddles
around kerosene lamps,
erasing corners.
Checkered oilcloth,
scrubbed pine counters
sagging a little
in their centers.

It's all coming back.
The big stove radiates heat,
wood hissing a little,
the coffeepot
that lives on the stove
puffs and bubbles.

There are so many smells:
coffee, wet wood and wool,
smoke, homemade soap,
kerosene and lampblack.

Uncle Gunnar and Uncle Odd
are planning a fishing trip.
They lean back
in the tipped oak chairs,
big men, unaware
of the miracle of their bodies.

Mom is playing cribbage with Dad.
They are intent,
pegs clicking in the holes,
wrapped in the light of the lamp.

For the next week
she will feed cows,
fill tinned pails
with foam-warm milk
while the men canoe
through the North Woods.

The light puddles in her eyes.

She is young.
She is still beautiful.

North Woods

SCALLOPED phone lines
edging winter fields hum.
White maned pines sigh,
creak like old bones.
Birches shake
in the impossible storms,
white bark peeling.
Old she-bear shifts
under her blanket of ice
and dreams of green leaves and honey.

Days are footprints in snow,
violet-shadowed holes
to fall into and out of.
Head down into the obstinate wind,
one plods on until cold
becomes solace.

In the short summers, frantic coupling
and uncoupling, memory of winter
imprinted. Husbands, lovers,
talk with their silence.
They slip quietly in,
and before first light are gone,
taking their gamey smell,
their tackle and wicker creels,

or 30-30s slung over their shoulders
for deer and moose.

Husbands roll over under stacks of quilts
to touch wives who have grown
as stiff as the starched dresses
frozen on their clotheslines,
flowered prints clacking.

Each year the lakes grow
hard and bitter,
and the children leave.

Dreaming the Pukak

"Pukak" is an Inuit word for an under-snow habitat

MAYBE IT WAS an imperceptible tilt
in the earth's axis, a shift
in the ocean currents, a blip
in the warm cycles between ice ages
that caused winters to be colder,
snow deeper then.

In the North Woods,
under the frozen bone of wind,
an ice crystal magic happens.
Water molecules migrate
from forest floor, leaving
a maze of tiny tunnels: the *pukak*.
Here shrews, mice, and voles live –
they would freeze quickly
in the open at 30 below.

Imagine snow-filtered light
cool and blue, silence broken
only by occasional footfalls,
muffled, dumb,
of some hungry predator,
little creatures
mostly safe below.

When a 22-foot drift
marooned us for weeks, I dug
corridors and caves in it –
a kind of large-scale *pukak*.
Grown-ups shoveled paths
higher than my head
to barn and outbuildings,
blue corridors of gloom
that kept drifting shut.

In closed rooms, stray curls
of wood smoke, overboiled cabbage,
urine and Vicks from sick Grandmother,
her tongue sharp as the lye soap Mama made.
Outside Grandma's door,
snow I turned my eyes from,
yellow, dimpled,
from tossed chamber pots.

Imagine, then, the freedom of skis or skates
when the temperature hit a tropical 15 below.
I never wanted to come in.
Often suffered frostbite on hands or chin,
cured by snow
packed hot as ashes on my skin.

Everything has its compensations.
When snowmelt left shallow lakes
on the snowpack and froze at 30 below,

I pretended they were canals in Holland,
skated for miles over fields, trailing
diaphanous scarves of breath.

In my dreams
Snow Queen was a shrew
stealing my fur-wrapped prince.
I would descend as a noble vole
to my make-believe *pukak*
to rescue him.
No howling winds,
only the tinkle
of falling ice crystals,
tiny feet scampering.

Yeats had his Lake Isle,
a kinder place.
I had what I was given.

Down-Home Cooking

IT'S NOT SURPRISING Mama was ample.
She cooked crisp-skin chicken
that melted down your chin,
goose with gooseberry sauce,
juicy free-range beef,
and fermented chokecherry wine
in great crocks
behind the woodstove.

On baking day, little tendrils of scent
tugged you from the best games
to hand-churned butter
over crunchy loaves,
cinnamon twists, caramel nut rolls,
and chocolate chip cookies
warm as a fat lap.

Toward the end of winter
we tired of our root crop and apples
molding toward slime in the cellar.
Home-canned vegetables looked bleached
as old bones in bottles.
Even Mama's magic couldn't make new
what was too old.
We wanted meat and found it,
when lucky, deep in the woods.

Once Uncle Gunnar
went hunting in the upper 40.
He was looking for deer or moose,
but found bear,
an angry early riser,
snow still quilting his lair.

Mama was an alchemist with game,
reasoned bear was the same.
She cut it into steaks.
The whole house smelled
of good meat cooking.
She and Gunnar grinned,
said nothing as we ate
around the big trestle table.
After Uncle Odd said "delicious"
and again "delicious"
and then once more –
which was one time too many –
Gunnar just had to tell him "bear."

"Bear," yelled Odd,
rearing up, knocking over his chair.
Ursine on hind legs,
the enormous rug
of his chest, claws,
the powerful jaws –
as if to become
what was taboo to eat.

Unlike Odd, we ate meat
for more than a week,
laughed at foolish Uncle,
who let his head
get in the way of his stomach.

Blacksmithing

FIRE THROBBED in the big fireplace
to the whoosh of foot-pedal bellows.
Dirt floor, sooty windows,
gritty coal-dust air.
Iron rods waited red hot –
iron to anvil, arc of hammer,
the room exploded, became sound,
then the hiss and shift of heat
to waiting water.
Again and again the room narrowed –
to noise, to black, to scarlet
of fire and iron, sparks flying,
Grandpa's muscles looking chipped
and glinting like steel.

It was a patient crafting,
the slow working to round
of a horseshoe,
horses outside waiting for the fit,
each tool the farm needed
done with perfect blows.
Sometimes he would give me a bar
to heat and hammer to an easy wedge,
would show me how,
so I could see with my hands
and the language of muscle

the measure of the craft –
how it stretched back
through thousands of years
and maybe that much forward.

We thought so then,
couldn't see
how we were at the end of a thing –
how everything would bend
right around
and go off a different way.

Queenie

SHE WAS AS MUCH a part of the view
as potato rows
that toed together in the distance
or the mounded rocks
that formed fences around the farm.

A tractor did her work now,
while she cropped grass
or stared into the distance,
dreaming, perhaps,
of teammates long dead,
or of frisking through the fields,
her life all juice and muscle.

The day I broke my bike
and rode Queenie bareback
five miles to Barbara's,
no slaps or press of heels could speed
her slow clopping. Steam
rose from her slick and lathered back,
and as she stumbled and swayed,
I flopped like a puppet across
the chain of hills that were her vertebrae.
I could almost hear Grandpa:
"That girl has to learn for herself,
and always the hard way."

At Barbara's I could hardly stand.
Queenie was a boat and I had sea legs.
What use was this old nag –
I might better have walked.

Then I thought of Grandpa,
of whisker rub and rough hug.
He'd allow no trip to the glue factory
for this horse. She'd hauled stones,
ploughed and tilled his soil,
her good work reaching back
through the years like seeds
rooting in the straight furrows she'd turned.
"Value unacknowledged," he said, "grows weeds."

Aunt Annie & Uncle Odd
Sing an Old Cowboy Song

DUST MOTES dance
in the slant light from the window
as if to the music of their two guitars.
And they are young, this brother and sister.
Their heads tilt together as they sing,
until Odd turns to the harmonica
and follows her voice,
the yodels tumbling
like water downstream.
Always I remember this stop-frame print,
the fragment of song.

Around it, the rest of the album:

Odd, brittling, cold
as the fish in lakes
where he's sawed holes,
always alone while he waits.
Snowshoes, harnesses,
hot breath of the horses
curling to frost in the air.
And at night the bottle,
followed by the whistle and rattle
of his snores.

Mom, slapping his face
with her wet dishrag,
then her sprawl
against the wall
where he's pushed her,
the violent blossom on her eye
unfolding its livid petals.

Annie, her words galloping
beyond comprehension,
talking to me for hours
about flowers on a card,
slipping on ice formed
between her and husband,
children, everything that was good.
Hard bit in the mouth,
the arched back,
volt after volt.

Always, I return to that cowboy song
to remember the beginning,
to remember
how I have loved them.

The Mole

UNCLE ODD AND I lie flat,
sun warming our upturned faces.
Plum leaves sway overhead,
quilting light.
Trumpet flowers blow
hot and brassy.

Gray goslings scurry around us
like downy potentates.
They pull at our clothes,
make soft honking sounds.

A puff of down
has found the big brown mole
on Uncle's face.
He begins to smile,
curiously gentle.

The gosling pulls and pulls,
pulls all that unhappiness out.
I think *yes* –
that's what moles are made for.

ƒitting In

HEAT hovers,
an ocher haze
over the pasture.
Cows bend to graze.
I yield to the slow
grinding of teeth,
the desultory
swish of tails.

This is the music of the field:
percussive brush of grass,
insect-buzzing baritones,
stamp of hoofs,
like trombones
the mournful moos.

Time slows.
This is too exquisite
to hold for more
than this minute.

I slip under the fence.
Uncropped grass,
cowslips, Queen Anne's lace,
buttercups.

I become four-legged,
full-uddered, thick,
slippery with sweat
and sweet milk.
Just inside the fence
a salt block, hollowed deep
where cows lick.

It's clean
on its vertical side.
I belly down to it,
lick like cows do –
everything coming
together, one,
the hollow in the salt
just fitting my tongue.

Deer Nature

THE CANOE glides,
a ghostly fish,
through white waters of fog.
From the boreal forest,
a long howl of wolves.
The lake mirrors a boat
and three men,
then offers up a fawn
to perplex them.
Exhausted, she swims close,
this island boat her only hope.

Dad and Gunnar lean away
to counterbalance Uncle Odd,
who wrestles her up to safety.
They paddle into camp,
the jack pine and cedar
looking sketched
in blue-black ink
that is bleeding
onto the paper-gray sky.

Night comes and constricts
to a circle of light,
these men, a fire, and a fawn.
Beyond them, the ancient balance:

hunter and hunted,
before the coming of the plow.

They fed her condensed milk
through a sock,
cut short their trip
and brought her home.
She became stunted to our way,
more dog than deer –
came to our call,
drank milk from a bottle,
followed us on walks.
I prefer to remember her
in our fields,
leaping through high grass
in the looping lines
of a fine calligrapher,
dogs hard at her heels.
The chase gave her back
her deer nature.

She wasn't with us long.
She learned to unhook any latch,
and hunting season
was relentless
as winter in Minnesota.

Felix of the Ojibwa

HE CAME, I am told, when the berries
were ripe and bending the staked vines.
I remember the tart sweetness, the heavy,
teasing scent, sun on arms, the thick
and sticky texture of those days.

I'm told I was crazy about him,
followed him around like a puppy.
But I remember him only from his photo –
the lean handsome grin,

his white shirt unbuttoned to the navel
like a flag on his dusky skin.
Around his neck, a sling
for holding up the box he used
for picking our raspberries.

Later, Aunt Liv told me
he'd married a girl from town
and moved to Saint Louis,
the charcoal streets closing down
on him, whiskey twisting the grin.
One night he cut up his wife
and with a gun he'd stolen,
took his own life.

The winter he left us
was the time of my terror of white,
each window opening out into it.
I crawled under the sills to remain unseen
and dreamed over and over
of free-falling from a mountain
to a whistle like a plane going down.
When I hit bottom, a tumble of stone.

Hay Harvest

WHEN A FEW GOOD DAYS lay before us
like a blessing, Uncle Gunnar
would take out the tractor
and the grass would swish down in waves
to the snap and slide of the mower.
It was forked over, dried
pale-yellow and pungent
and raked into rows by arching tines
pulled behind the Farmall.

We children followed,
pitched rows into stacks,
then the hayrack
like a bed – no sides –
a man on top to make a load,
two below to fork a stack
in easy rhythm.
All of us drunk on scent: hay,
subtones of sweat,
and the yeasty smell
of beer at breaks.

Back at the barn,
load tucked under the big hay door,
the forklift would bite in,
then pull the hay up,

click onto the rail inside the roof peak
and ride to its drop point,
the great hayloft filling with miles
of those threads of sun,
seeds and dust swirling.

Haying far fields was best:
long rides back,
swaying and slow on the springy load,
tractor straining.

On night rides,
lying flat on prickly softness,
the Bears and Orion straddling
impenetrable distances –
anything seemed possible,
the entire Milky Way
up there just for us,
year after generous year.

*L*ost

for Wesley

THESE were not
our familiar summer woods.
We were lost,
blizzard-wrapped.
White of sky
and ground and eye.
Sounds of breath and heartbeat
separating from silence
as if it were the whole
of existence.

Tree limbs like old bones
creaked with white weight
as we did, lurching like drunks
through thigh-high drifts.

We didn't dare rest –
old Norse stories
of falling asleep and freezing
rose from the snowpack
in Grandpa's voice.

We crossed and recrossed
our footprints,
measured time

by the snow that filled them.
Hemlocks, pines, birches –
mere brush strokes
on a vast blank canvas.

Our thoughts spun
like blown snow
until something took over
and we could just go,
moving first one leg
then the other,
each with its own place
in time –
time itself sheering away
into featureless white.

Uncle Odd

THE HARD FACT OF HIS LIFE he learned early: winter. How winter defined things, smoothed over, erased. It was cold, yes, but that was challenge, and it was easily seen. Wind, ice, snow left few places to go. He got used to minimum: few words, straightforward action, quick downhill runs on skis, no lift to ease the climb back up.

There was a longing, I know there was. I remember his head pressed against the cows' bellies crooning old ballads while he milked. He could gentle any cranky cow, but humans defeated him. His mother – my grandmother – so sour and withdrawn. Had she ever held him, crooned to him? I think he took something of each hard winter into the abundance of summer, but maybe that was after the war.

Maybe before the war he'd walked under a drift of apple blossoms and spun around in delight, pressed his nose into narcissus and rose. I didn't know him then, but I can imagine him later on skis,

schussing down some alpine slope, distant fire puffing the
snow, the muffled explosions coming that second or so
later. The surprise when that bit of lead entered him, the
trail of fire, the pain almost a relief because it got him out.
And he must have been hopeful then: he had this girl to
go back to, carried her picture – an inside-pocket girl.

It would have been winter. Maybe if it had been summer,
things would have been different, he might have taken
it better: her gone, married to another. Maybe the ice
wouldn't have settled so heavily into all those unmelting
places – glacial scrapings, the hard unyielding soil.
Later she had come to him, said it was a mistake. If it had
been summer, he might not have said he wouldn't take
used goods. He might have looked out on the grasses,
braided with buttercups and waving in the wind, and
been softened.

Afterward, there was his life – so much snow falling,
drifting over fields and fences, obliterating definition. Oh,
there were melts each spring, but the summers were short.
Sometimes in late August, the first snow. And there were
no women. I wonder at how perfectly Odd moved into his
name. Did he make her leaving the central fact of his life?
I think he did. I think she became mother and deserter,
packed into one small snowball that picked up speed and
size as it rolled with him all the way down to the bottom.

Uncle Odd & the Three Bears

HE WAS mending fences
in the far forty. A watery sun,
barbed wire coiled
like three snakes
on the barely thawed soil.

He moved between two
posts, empty
and ready for new wire,
he turned,
bent to grab a coil
and saw the bears
coming full gallop.
That's when
he first understood Einstein –

how the gravity of terror
can bend and slow time.
Muzzles narrowing to nose,
those tiny eyes –
three mountains,
three great lumbering weights
coming straight toward him!

Still, a part of him remembered:
drop to the ground face down.

It took forever
but they passed,
wanting only
a way out,
that break in the fence.

Einstein returned to the shelf,
Odd's life wheeled back,
the snapped-shut doors
swung open again,
day resumed its tick.

He left wire and fence
where they were, needing time –
now given back to him
and infinitely precious –
to mend.

Wash Day

WHEN SCENT of Mama's split pea soup
threaded its fingers into my room,
I knew it was wash day,
pearly light of the unrisen sun
illuminating the edges
of bed and dormer ledge.

Downstairs, Mama had been busy
for hours –
circle of heat
from the woodstove,
windows white with steam,
first tubs of water boiling.
She would give me oatmeal
with honey and foamy milk
still warm from the cow.

After breakfast, my first trips
to the well: smooth ash
of the yoke arched
to fit my neck, curved
to fit my shoulders –
Grandpa's careful carpentry.

I'd hook a pail to each side,
walk to the end of the drive,

then quick pumps
before the water lifted.
When it came,
it took the weight of my body
to bring the handle down.
Always the last look in:
deep, dark as death.
A stone bounced
side to side,
over and over,
before the splash,
I, safe up top.

In the kitchen, from paired tubs,
steam twisted to angel shapes,
or so I imagined.
In one tub the scrub board
and homemade lye soap –
Mama bent over it,
her heat-polished face
penny shiny. She'd rub, swish,
twist to wring,
then into the second tub,
rinse, a hard twist,
and into the basket.

Out at the line, she'd bend,
lift, pin, bend, lift, pin,
the flap and snap of clothes,

smell of sun and soap
subduing the scent
that lived on the lawn – grass,
damp earth, and always,
and over everything, pine:
the great Norways circling
the house like a chorus of crones,
dark-robed, protective.

I loved this work.
But what of Mama?
Maybe if she could
have stopped yearning
for a man as intent
on his family
as on saving the world,

if she could have savored
the ritual, the smell,
gentled her mind,
taken each part of the day
in its own time –
maybe then
she could have loved it.

Hard Labor

WHEN I REMEMBER Uncle Gunnar,
I see him stripped to the waist,
sun winking
from wet muscles, tossing forkfuls
of sweet hay. Or milking
on his sawed-off stool,
head pressing a cow's belly.
He'd croon and soothe
and two-finger tug those long teats,
playing soprano milk-notes
against a tinned pail.

Or I see his green boots
hip deep
in some trout stream,
arm lifted
to conduct his line,
which snaked its hissing song
over the surface.

He wasn't, like Grandpa,
given to talk and stories,
but he was steady.
Something needed,
he got it.

One Minnesota winter,
tall winds raking snow
to the roofs,
we needed food.
No money, and we needed food.
Gunnar set out on snowshoes,
the 30-30 slung on his shoulder.

He tracked a deer clear
to the edge of Sederquist's land.
We always thought Lefty Sederquist
heard the shot and snitched.

The game warden caught Gunnar
yoked to a makeshift deer-drag.
The judge gave him the work farm –
58 days of hard labor,

subzero winds howling
out of the north.
Like the law.

Driving Lesson

OURS WAS a stately promenade:
the great wagon like a bed
but with foot and head
rising eight feet from the floor
and swaying down the scythed rows.
A scene old as farming,
but with Queenie out to pasture,
now the rig was pulled by a tractor.

The men move in spirals,
raking hay into stacks,
regular, smooth as dance.
Two men at each
sweet-scented pile
toss hay in an arc
to the man on top
shaping the load.

It's a long way to the barn.
Clouds are spreading
their dark robes.
It will rain.

Every man is needed.
Female and eleven years,
I'm given the tractor.

From the edge of the seat
my feet barely touch
the pedals.
A quick lesson,
and when I grind gears –
yells.

I suppose they overloaded it.
This was all they'd get
before the storm hit.

Climbing a steep hill,
the load too heavy,
front tires lift
off the ground.
Higher and higher,
I'm flapping
from the wheel like a flag –
20 degrees more
and the tractor
will flip backward.
Men jumping
on front and sides
like frogs to a pond,
until the wheels come down.

They didn't apologize.
They laughed, pounded chests,
shouted aloud and taught me

by what they did,
not what they said:
to look at the best,
let the rest veer away.

Fifteen

IT WAS the time
of the poured honey of skin,
unstubbled cheeks.
Our fingers
little nibbling fish,
smelt or grunion.
We waded in hip boots,
cold seeping through rubber.
Tire fires, seine nets,
milk cans filled
with the slap of silver.

Fish fried under a moon's wink
vied with rumpled blankets,
sand, the hot untried
bodies wanting to know,
aching for a path in or out,
the wild reaching.

We couldn't see
how beautiful we were:
you lifting like the moccasin flower
from our ordinary earth,
stamen and stalk;
me, oyster tender
inside my shell,

my small breast
opening to your tongue,
the innocence of nipple.

We could have done anything.
We were so young.

The earth sighed and settled,
pressing out a few agates,
but mostly the plain stones.
Black flies came in great clouds
biting through clothes.
Mosquitoes wheeled and hummed,
everything
digging down under us.

How I Remember

I REMEMBER so clearly
the height of my hand,
the exact triangle of the bent arm,
twist of my body
that almost lengthened
the angle to line.
The shock of the stop as I hit him.
Something held down too long
  let loose, thrust up, shot out,
    unexpected,
      a stranger,
        an unthinking bone.

I was fifteen and smitten,
can't remember why I slapped him
so long ago,
but I do remember
  the snap of my neck,
    the hundred needles,
      the precise arc
        of the return blow.

$\mathcal{A}$n Intelligence of Crows

In New Caledonia, moneduloides crows strip leaves and bark from twigs, nip them at their base to make hooks, and snip toothed leaves from pandanus plants to probe or rake bugs from holes. Even the much-studied chimp has never been seen making planned implements.

THEY ARE gathering again
on the ponderosas
that line the road.
Raucous, untidy, they flap
with some grace,
but plop down
heavy as thrown stones.

Not an admired bird –
others are a *flock*,
they are a *murder* –
and we write them
into our dark poems.

I had a pet crow.
Fed him worms
that made his breath
like an outhouse on a hot day.
Felix loved jewelry and mischief.
His nest was a jangle
of bright bangles,
and he unpinned Mom's wash
more than once.

He would fly to a safe branch,
cackle until she came out.
She swore that crow would laugh
at each curse and rehung shirt.

I never saw Felix carve tools,
but he picked beans with Mom,
placed each one
carefully in her basket.
Like a show-off child
proud of a new trick,
he offered to pick
for most of our neighbors.

He flew while I walked,
landing on my raised arm
with all the charm
of a bumbling adolescent.

At home, he tugged ears,
groomed my hair.

That curl of matter
that makes us who we are
curls as elegantly
through other living things.

And I see no sign of murder,
only a smart, cacophonous tribe
blossoming
on an enormous tree.

Fresh Off the Farm

SEVENTEEN in Chicago:
the guys, cigarettes
rolled up in sleeves,
smooth talking,
all wanting me.
This South Side
like a foreign country.

There was no TV
on the farm. What we knew
stepped out of stories
or the simple days
we lived through.

But I loved the lights.
Back home we'd barely
gone beyond kerosene;
here the stars
were plucked from the sky
and stuck on stores
like rhinestones.

On Cottage Grove, the shops
wore their best neon scarves.
Woolworth's, the Roxie,
lights running little races

around the marquee.
Those few blocks,
a world to watch.

One night, walking back
from the glitter,
summer, little breeze breaths,
looking at the flutter
of curtains, open windows,
back stoops in rows,
zigzag steps into the dark –
why didn't I hear him?

At my door, a push
from behind –
cold steel, the mail slots
slammed to my face,
turned round to
the boiled cabbage smell
of a rough embrace.

If he hadn't thrust
a warm salami-tongue
deep into my mouth,
I might not have –
but he did,
so almost as if
I had no choice –
my mother's voice

echoing from an old story –
I clamped my teeth down,
as she had: hard, extreme,
the soft flesh giving way,
and, beginning in the throat –
was it his? mine?
both entwined? –
that feral scream.

fire

THE HOUSE creaked and gasped,
released from the last freeze
by a balmy 30 degrees.
Sigmund Einbu lay dreaming
under mounds of fraying quilts
made by mother and sisters,
layered remnants of family stories,
pieced dresses and ties
cross-stitched and forgotten.

He had left the farm behind,
but for what? Cigars, a suit,
no children, a marriage
bitter as the chokecherry wine
he could never make right.
Here he was, pushing nine decades,
alone and back where he'd started.

Outside, barn and outbuildings
wore white caps,
the sharp edges of stacked
wood lay smoothed by snow
and silvered under a snipped moon.

So beautiful,
yet the old farm

seemed empty as an echo
under its white sheet.
His, the only heartbeat
left here, right over the furnace,
which was sending heat
like breath
through the scrolled vents.

Strange, how everyone seemed
more real, now that they had left him.
They walked at night in his dreams
full-colored and fleshed,
puzzle pieces
searching for their place.
Why wouldn't they leave him?
So many brothers and sisters,
the reasons for their lives
forever a mystery.

What had it all come to?
Everything weathers away.
You open an old nut
and it's hollow inside,
the spark that made it grow
gone. Still, there was the land,
open to him,
plowed in his dreams.

In the furnace,
a few hungry logs flared,
caked wood ash
from a thousand fires
took hold in the chimney, reached
through chipped mortar
to the attic, its boxes
of forlorn leavings. Then down
to the four bedrooms,
Sigmund still sleeping
near the kitchen below.

It licked through mounds
of sister Annie's clothes
left piled on every bed,
from when she'd slept
each night in a different room.

Why hadn't he been alarmed
when last year
for two days
she hadn't come downstairs?
A diabetic coma, broken arm –
she was safe now,
removed to a nursing home.

If the sigh of wood as it caught
echoed her old lament,

Sig didn't hear. He slept on
until the upstairs
was mostly gone.

He dialed 911,
yelled *Fire!*
and the connection snapped.

What was there to keep him?
Surely the body,
which never wavers,
fought on.
There was no one left now
to take him up
but the flames.

What Is Written

for my mother, Bryn

1.

IN THE PHOTO enormous elms
press the sky,
but, in the distance, they recede
to pencil strokes
the size of the plaid of Mother's coat.
Hair permed, heels, a cloche hat.
It's 1935. Possibility,
like the sidewalk,
opens out before her.
What is past
is written in pages of snow
that have melted away.

I have not read them but know
she moved through the swirl
of detail from some still point
that let her delight
in marsh grass, buttercup,
three-leaf clover, because luck
was a harder thing to find.

Duty bent her
to pay the mortgage,
her dream of school vanishing

year after year with the snow.
She sent her sisters,
though she couldn't go,
then made her escape:
marriage, children,
a few good years, I hope,
smooth as her ironed sheets.

Then Grandpa came
with Grandma, who was palsied
and clearly on the way down.
Who else to nurse her
but Mom, the oldest.
I was eleven
when we returned.

2.

MOM, I REMEMBER the music
of that time:
high-pitched whines
from your sick mother
confined you
as if to a box of gears
meshing note to note,
everything rote.

While I roamed
buttercup-drunk,
you canned, soaped plates,

cleaned bedpans.
While I watched wind part clouds,
sang children's songs aloud,
you boiled water
on the old woodstove,
churned butter, ironed clothes.

Again and again,
you laid your body down
like a stone
for me to step on.
I wish I had been able to see
before it was too late –
not for me, for your sake.

We Have the Gift

WHEN I WAS BORN, Mama, silent as slate
for a year, finally sent a letter
the length of two states back home.
When Grandma walked
the half-mile to the mailbox,
Aunt Liv knew before she opened it –
said, "Bryn's got married and had a girl!"

Formed by the dark
earth unfolding behind the plow,
Liv's mind – thick as woods
with bird life, bear,
the slidings of soft-nosed deer
shadow to shadow –
lifted out past the edges of thought.
Later, she would see moose,
the pronged plates of their antlers;
would tell husband Harvey
where to go to find them
and how many bullets to use.

Decades later, I told her of slipping
into another lifetime – seeing it
in reflected light like a fat moon
on a black lake – half-timbered cottage,

rammed earth floor,
scent of death like old potatoes.

And the time in the shower:
premonition, my son in danger –
I leapt out, spraying water on the run
to the window, pressed the notion
away, only to jump out again
and find him crying.
On his head, the tipped ink

of a bruise blooming.
Liv wasn't surprised – we had *the gift*.

Last year she dreamed
of Uncle Sig on a funeral pyre.
Well, he's old, she thought.
A week later, flames fought
with aging timbers,
the old homestead lost.
Sig burned at the window,
arms out,
reaching.

When could we ever change things?
Mostly we watched,
impotent,
touched with a gift
from gods who were playful
but indifferent.

Beavers

ONCE, YOU COULD paddle a canoe
on chains of blue lakes
that lay, as if carelessly tossed,
across a thousand miles of wilderness.
Beaver dams shortened portages,
let in the fur trade's big York boats,
let in hunters, until
the dams lay like tangled graves,
and the streams became shallow.

One summer I found a dam
on our creek. Beavers
must have come down linked lakes
from the North Woods.
I thought they were gone forever,
a few dusty hats their only legacy.
We were on the edge of things –
everything south
neatly squared and peopled,
the north uncharted
bramble and log tumble.

That summer I was their secret admirer.
Saw them fell a small willow
in five minutes,
build their dam helter-skelter,

branches and logs mud-chinked.
Mostly, I heard just the tail-slap warning,
or saw slicked fur heads
dive to safety.

Uncle Gunnar said
they had to keep chewing
or their teeth would grow so long
they'd curl right around
and pierce their brains.
He'd always explain
how nature turned mean
when her gifts weren't used.

Their mounded lodge
was an island in the pond,
the pond an island in the woods
graced by lilies and burr reeds.
Still water breeds sawflies and mosquitoes:
frog and ruffed-grouse food.
Beaver-made habitat,
my fascinating strangers in the water.

The beavers had five fine years
before young Butch Swenson
got good enough with his 30-30.
By then I'd stopped watching.
By then I'd turned south.

Boundary Waters

THE CANOE whispers to the water.
Drops from each oar answer,
breaking silence like breath.

Above, blue sky,
a few curls of cloud,
below, the complex dark web
of water life.
We're skimming along
on the thinnest of illusions:
what is over us
reflected from beneath us
as if it were all there is.

The canoe is at home here.
Years ago, Grandpa made it
from paper birch.
He learned how
from an old Chippewa.

Shadows point their long fingers.
We nose onto an island,
its flat granite ledge.
Gather sphagnum and feather moss
for our bed,
wood, birch bark for kindling.

We fish for dinner, singing,
"Oh Mother, now I feel lucky,
give me a muskie big and husky,"
connecting this time to the *all time*
that flows around us.

Our fire carves a room
out of the night
before the moon's rising.
From the other shore, wolves,
their mournful *ah-oo ah-oo.*

Morning. A new fire,
coffee thick enough to stand on,
and we're back on the lake,
floating in and out of puffs of mist –
cool breath of the old gods –
lit up now,
but thinned by time.

We paddle onto a stream
straddled by birch and aspen.
Behind them, the boreal forest,
home of the North Wind, shadows
of ancient brothers,
an immense dark roof
of spruce and pine.

Beavers have widened the creek
with their tangle of dams.
In the beaver pond,
water lily, bulrush, a fat leech
curled on the bottom.

A short portage,
another lake.
Glaciers gouged these out
by the thousands.
We could paddle to Pigeon River,
Thunder Bay, or up
to Lake Winnipeg,
like generations of Chippewa.

I dip my oar in water and pull,
a hard stroke, perfect,
familiar – my body remembers
when it was brown-skinned
and brave.
It knows so perfectly
what to do.

Wilburn Bryan Wells

WHEN I WAS YOUNG, my father was most real in the elegant angle of his prose on crisp and folded paper postmarked Chicago, Madison, Peoria.

Who he was, was about other places. I imagine them, mountains shouldering a little town, cool sun struggling over the peaks and vanishing scant hours later. A silver-mining town, turn of the century. Streets of mud or dust or ice.

In musty photographs yellowing in cardboard boxes, in the ordered albums from the farm, mostly he is missing. He appears here and there as if cut from another place and pasted – an elegant bony frame, city hat.

He was handsome, thin as shadow. And tough, had to be – thrown out of his home by his father at thirteen.

It was 1910. He hit the rails, wintered with the bums in
Pismo Beach. They shared food, cooked in oil cans over
open fires, kept each other alive. Lived like rats, at the edge
of things, wanting to bring it all down. Were called
Wobblies.

Dad sang their songs like a kid learning to ride a bike –
lurching outside the melody. He sang of strikes and of
strike-breakers, altered church hymns:

> *Longhaired preachers come out every night,*
> *try to tell you what's wrong and what's right.*
> *But when you ask them for something to eat,*
> *they will answer in voices so sweet:*
> *You will eat, by and by,*
> *in that glorious land up in the sky, way up high,*
> *work and pray, live on hay,*
> *you'll get your pie in the sky when you die.*

Daddy said the railroad bulls carried guns, clubs – and used
them. He saw the world from boxcars, from between the
tracks, beneath rubber hoses that came down on his back
in jail rooms. He never could settle – or the FBI wouldn't
let him.

First a Wobbly, then a Communist. He named me after
Ella Reeve Bluer, labor leader. Mom hid the *Communist
Manifesto, Das Kapital,* all the *Daily Worker*s under

floorboards in the chicken coop, afraid they'd be found. But oh, she believed. This was the new religion, his church the labor unions. His service, recruiting, organizing in towns in Wisconsin, Minnesota, Illinois.

Later we joined him. In 1948, rallies – Henry Wallace for President. I was ten. Banners and balloons, scratch-voiced songs. Party bigwigs in our living room. I sat on Gus Hall's lap. Talk, like carnival lights, dazzled us. It all seemed so simple, so right.

Then Dad got too well known. Towns became revolving doors – he went in, was driven out. And we moved and moved. For my brother it was easy, but I was always just settling in. . . .

Dad felt the end justified the means, but what of the Gulag, the millions dead? News leaked like sewage onto all the clean white carpets. His last years bent him like a question, hours spent hunched over newspapers, searching for discrepancies, hoping to prove it all a lie.

I saw that. What he gave me was fear of easy answers and *isms.* Though I loved the father, it's taken this long to love the boy who climbed those early peaks, the man who wanted to make things better, who wouldn't settle for dusty streets in some tired town.

The Old Einbu Farm

GRANDPA BUILT the barn,
the gabled clapboard house,
all the buildings on the farm –
the blacksmith shop, carpentry shop,
chicken coop, root cellar, windmill.
He designed them, he raised them,
he nailed them.

What Grandma raised
were nine children.
Three others died.
Six had children
who sometimes lived here,
the old homestead humming –
a sound sometimes joyful,
sometimes quarrelsome –
steady, seemingly, as stone.

But we were
children of our era,
scattered like shot
across the States.

Now, the buildings settle
in the landscape
like unplaced puzzle pieces.

Buttercups, grasses, Queen Anne's lace
flow around them in the wind like water.
Our hill road vanished
beneath waist-high weeds.

Up close, you see the slippage
in peeling patches of paint,
in cobwebs linking harnesses, tackle,
old scythes to stanchions,
the chicken coop tipping
off its foundation.

Through the unwashed
wavy-glassed window:
Aunt Annie and Uncle Sig,
grown dry and cracked
as late autumn grass.
They sit in the dim kitchen
at the not-so-scrubbed table
and blink, their teeth soaking
in chipped cups by the sink.

When I enter to talk,
we hardly know how.
They only want to play pinochle.

I want to brush my hand
over their once-familiar hair,
but I stop.

It's finished.
My place in the homestead
is lost.

American Gothic

MOTHER, you painted this land
with a hand so strong,
only now that you are gone
can I begin to see
where your brush has touched me.

And here I am, returning
to what you struggled to leave:
country of glacial scrapings,
winters of tight-buttoned
white coats, drudge
of scrub and plant and churn.
Like a donkey forever circling
a grinding stone,
you never unyoked yourself.

I speed up at the SLOW sign,
leave the blacktop to bounce
on scrub-board ruts
of gravel-gone-mud-gone-gravel,
swing right at the mailbox
onto Evans – should be Einbu – Road
(after 70 years of Einbus here,
we should have changed the name).

Ahead, *American Gothic*
ringed by crabapple. Here you knelt
to the unforgiving god of order,
gave him the tender
branch of your body.

I park the rented Ford.
The house stands
but softens like an apple
toward mold.
Outbuildings sag
on their foundations.

What has all your work come to,
exuberance of life left
only in fields unleashed to weed?

The thousand small jobs
that order a day
tear at me like brambles
when I try
to prune them away.

Where does what we've left reside,
that it can't
by a simple act of will
be set aside?

What You Wanted

for Barbara

WE WERE so young,
talking for hours
as we lay on your roof,
The deep bowl of stars
turning around us
as if we were true north,
as if we were center.
Up there,
anything seemed possible,
when by day
our path curved out of sight
just beyond the trees.

Your girlish dreams
were cut from magazines –
dark slash of lips,
nylon seams straight as
what you wanted:
slick picture on the page –
men in the foreground,
unbuttoned shirts,
hair nipped to ducktails.
Tracks of their cars
scoring your yard.

I was a farm girl, tuned
to the rhythm
of crop and season,
breasts mostly idea.
My fantasies hadn't yet
turned past necking.
I thought you'd always have
a man's arm tight
around your waist,
and in your mouth
the taste of many men.
And for a while you did.

We lost touch,
but a decade later
I found you married
to a local boy.
His bottles lay strewn
across your ruined landscape.
Reverberations of his Harley
amplified in the packed
houses of your street.
I could barely look
at the parched fields
of your face, collapsed
and capillary-traced.
Your talk turned mean
as your rooms.

That was after university
but before I married
and moved to Europe,
following ancient roads
that curved out of sight
past tilted houses bright
with red geraniums.

How strange that it was I,
not you,
writing, sipping
a rich, dark brew
in those cafés,
conversations spilling over
into the streets.

Old friend, though I wanted
you with me, we spun off
to different galaxies.
I measured our distance
when you looked down
from some cold
and distant star and said,
"Marry a Jew,
Ella, how could you?"

*E*nclosures

SUN PRESSES the fields dry.
Rows of corn bend to their own shade.
The sky reaches all the way around
to touch the ground on every side,
enclosing the farmer
and his carefully tended fields,
and the wife,
who encloses the farmer and the children
in the rectangles
of her carefully tended home.

A car shoots like a comet on its path
through the geometry of the field,
enclosing a driver, his wife and children
in the algebra of its movement.
They are cool and contained,
their radio turned up.

They don't see the farmer –
the perfectly drawn shape of his life –
and he doesn't see theirs.
They don't see the sprinkler,
pipes arching up and down
over the field like a centipede,
water whooshing.

They don't hear the sigh of thirsty corn
or see the gorgeous black beetle bathing.

Waiting

IN THE FARMHOUSE coatroom,
boots tipped like bent cornstalks
line the wall and drip water
that becomes a flow of ice
as it slips out the door.

A wheedling wind intrudes.
The kitchen stove hisses and pops,
heats the face but leaves the back
to the nipped chill – a taste
of what waits in the cold hands
of unheated rooms.

Grandmother rocks and rocks,
dour, predictable
as the ticking of her clock.

I remember the girl I was,
reading in a halo of light
from the kerosene lamp,
summer a fragment of dream –
a touch on my tongue of strawberry,
rhubarb dipped in a pocket of sugar.
Or an elusive scarf of scent –
cut grass or peonies or cow pancakes,
pungent and steaming.

But reality was winter,
the choke
of wood smoke, stale tobacco,
rutabagas boiling up, cloying.
I refused to eat them
no matter what they said.

Outside, snow drifted
across the porch, lifted
to touch a window,
glass iced
into twisted silvered scenes
like daguerreotypes
or early magazines.

And beyond the front door,
waiting like a question,
the unplowed road to explore.

Acknowledgments

MY THANKS to the many fine poets in Marin, for the love of the craft of poetry they share with me and for the community they provide. Special thanks to Robin Jacobson, who suggested this book, then prodded me to complete it. Thanks to Burr Overstreet, who inspires me with his courage and dazzles me with his wonderful weave of words, and to Marie Henry and Arlene Stark, whose critical insight I so admire.

Thanks to Tom Centolella, who has been my mentor for many years and who listened patiently when I could barely tie together a poem. Thanks also to other teachers along the way: Dorianne Laux, Jackie Kudler, Stefanie Marlis, and Diana O'Hehir.

Other poets who have shared their work with me have been invaluable: Dolores de Leon, Suzanne Himmelwright, Ann Goldsmith, Louise Murphy, Lola Brown, Judith Stephens, Sara Barbieri, Valle Brokes, Mary Haynes. The list goes on, but don't we all influence one another?

Then there is Jean Pumphrey, who was my co-chair at the Marin Poetry Center. She has always been firmly in my corner. I can never thank her enough. With Jean, creating new directions for the Poetry Center was satisfying and fun. And what a board of directors we had! Thanks to them all.

Finally, my family: To my husband, Matt, for his patient vetting of my poems and his steady support and appreciation. My children, Elana and David, for insights when I have struggled with a concept or a way to enter the material. And, of course, those who inspired this book, the generations of my family in Minnesota – my brother, my parents, and my aunts, uncles, and grandparents.

Haying the far fields

WAS EDITED, DESIGNED & PRODUCED by Robin Jacobson for True North Press, the literary imprint of Fulcrum Media Services, San Anselmo, California

ILLUSTRATED with photographs from the poet's family albums

COMPOSED in Bembo, a Monotype font based on typefaces cut by Francesco Griffo (c. 1450–1518, Italy) for a book by Pietro Bembo, and in Bernhard Tango, which was designed by Lucian Bernhard (1883–1972, Germany)

AND PRINTED & BOUND IN AN EDITION OF 500 COPIES on Sappi Lustro and Fox River Coronado, acid-free, recycled papers, by DeHart's Printing Services in Santa Clara, California.